The Oneidas

by Audrey Stansbury

HOUGHTON MIFFLIN   BOSTON

PHOTOGRAPHY CREDITS: **Cover** The New York Public Library/Art Resource, NY. **Title page** © FOTOSEARCH RM/age fotostock **3** The Granger Collection, New York. **5** Photodisc/Getty. **8** The New York Public Library/Art Resource, NY. **10** Painting by Don Troiani, www.historicalimagebank.com. **11** © Lee Snider/Photo Images/CORBIS. **12** © FOTOSEARCH RM/age fotostock **14** Karl Weatherly/Getty Images.

Printed in China

ISBN-13: 978-0-547-02570-4
ISBN-10: 0-547-02570-X

13 14 15 16 0940 19 18 17 16
4500569761

Table of Contents

Introduction

During the winter of 1777, members of the Continental Congress gathered for a meeting. There, American leaders made a special promise. This promise was made to the first group of people to fight alongside the colonists in the Revolutionary War. This group had already helped the colonists win important victories against the British.

The grateful Congress promised, "While the sun and moon continue to give light to the world, we shall love and respect you. As our trusty friends, we shall protect you."

Who were these friends whom the Congress promised to respect and protect? They were the Oneidas, an American Indian nation.

The Continental Congress met regularly during the Revolutionary War.

3

The Americans had a good reason to feel grateful. The Oneidas had joined the ranks of the American army. They had fought alongside the colonists in their struggle against the British. The Oneidas' bravery helped win important battles.

But after the war, the Congress did not keep its promise of friendship and protection. The Oneidas' vital contributions to America's freedom were largely forgotten. The Indian nation suffered greatly.

This is the story of the Oneidas, forgotten heroes of the Revolutionary War.

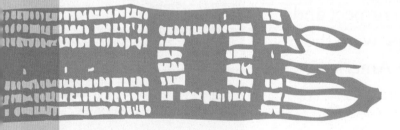

The People of the Standing Stone

The Oneidas called themselves "the People of the Standing Stone." They lived in North America for many hundreds of years before Europeans arrived. They inhabited about six million acres. Their lands were located in what is now New York State and northern Pennsylvania.

In Oneida villages, women grew squash, corn, and beans. They also gathered firewood and raised children. Men hunted and fished. Food was shared among the entire community.

Oneida Clans

The Oneida Nation was made up of three different *clans*, or groups—Bear, Turtle, and Wolf. The animal symbol of each clan represented a different trait that Oneida culture valued. The Bear represented gentleness and strength. The Turtle stood for patience and persistence. The Wolf represented strong family ties.

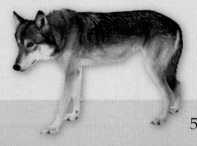

The People of the Long House

The Oneidas belonged to a group of five Indian nations—Mohawk, Onondaga, Cayuga, Seneca, and Oneida. These five nations protected each other from outside enemies. They settled internal disagreements through discussion. Together, they called themselves "the People of the Long House." European settlers called them the "Iroquois (IR uh kwoi) League."

By banding together, the five nations became powerful. They were able to protect their lands. They also dealt successfully with European settlers. Beginning in the 1600s, they made treaties with Dutch, French, and British colonists.

The People of the Long House controlled a large area of land in what is now New York State.

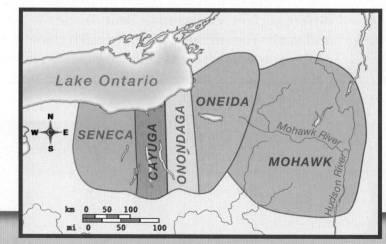

Caught in the Middle

When the Revolutionary War began, the People of the Long House found themselves in a difficult position. They were caught between the colonists and the British. Both groups wanted the five nations' skilled warriors to fight for their side.

For a long time, the Oneidas and the other Indian nations remained neutral. But eventually, they were forced to choose a side.

People of the Mohawk, Onondaga, Cayuga, and Seneca nations favored the British. There were several reasons. The British promised to respect their lands. They also gave them European provisions, such as muskets, ammunition, and cloth.

But the Oneidas felt loyal to their American friends. As a people who valued freedom, the Oneidas understood why the colonists were fighting. They sympathized with the Americans' desire to break free from British rule.

After much discussion, the Oneidas decided to fight for the Americans. The other nations decided to fight for the British. These decisions split the People of the Long House. The split had tragic consequences. In the Revolutionary War, the Oneidas found themselves fighting against brother warriors from the Mohawk, Onondaga, Cayuga, and Seneca nations.

Two Great Warriors

Skenandoah was an influential Oneida warrior known for his intelligence and courage. In 1775, he met with General George Washington to discuss the colonists' struggle against the British. Washington later noted that Skenandoah was "an Oneida Chief of considerable Rank" whose nation "ha[d] been very friendly to the Cause of the United Colonies." Skenandoah's meeting with Washington strengthened the Oneidas' friendship with the Americans.

Skenandoah

The Battles of Fort Stanwix and Oriskany

By the summer of 1777, the Oneidas had officially joined the American side. But the war was not going well for the colonists. The British had just captured Fort Ticonderoga, an American base in northeastern New York.

Then in mid-July, an Oneida warrior known as Thomas Sinavis arrived at American army headquarters. He had just returned from a secret scouting mission in Canada. He had been spying on British troops stationed there.

In Canada, Sinavis learned valuable information about British war plans. He told the Americans that the British were going to attack Fort Stanwix, an important American stronghold in New York. Sinavis had also learned the exact date of the planned British attack.

Sinavis strongly urged the Americans to fight. "Now is your time, brothers… defend and save your country before it is too late," he said.

The Americans listened to Sinavis's advice. When the British attacked the fort, they were ready. Many Oneida warriors fought, too. They helped drive off the British and save Fort Stanwix.

Oneidas also fought at the bloody Battle of Oriskany on August 6, 1777. Han Yerry Tewahangarahken, a warrior of the Wolf clan, was one of the heroes at Oriskany. Even after he was shot, Han Yerry kept fighting, using his tomahawk with great dexterity. His wife and son also fought in the battle.

The Oneidas fought bravely alongside the Americans at the Battle of Oriskany.

Saratoga: A Decisive Victory

In the fall of 1777, Oneida warriors fought at the Battle of Saratoga. This was a decisive American victory. Saratoga turned the tide of the war in the colonists' favor.

Battle of Saratoga Monument

Oneidas were involved in many aspects of this victory. They captured prisoners and spied on the enemy. They also conducted surprise attacks on British forces. These raids terrified enemy troops. The constant threat of Oneida attacks made it hard for the British to get much-needed supplies.

Valued Allies

Throughout the war, the Oneidas supported the Americans. They fought in many battles. They went on dangerous scouting missions. American commanders valued the Oneidas for their courage, knowledge, and honesty.

Polly Cooper

The winter of 1777–1778 was long and hard. George Washington's troops were camped at Valley Forge, Pennsylvania, where they had little food.

In April 1778, a group of Oneidas traveled more than 250 miles to Valley Forge. They brought corn for the hungry Americans. An Oneida known as Polly Cooper made a nourishing corn soup for the soldiers.

General Washington and the troops were very grateful to Polly Cooper for her generous act. In thanks, Washington's wife, Martha, gave Polly a beautiful shawl. The shawl still exists today.

This statue honors the Oneidas' role in the Revolutionary War. The statue is in the Museum of the American Indian in Washington, D.C.

After the War

When the Oneidas returned home after the war, they found devastation. Their villages had been destroyed. Their families were scattered.

But the worst was still to come. The Oneidas were poor and vulnerable, and many people wanted their valuable land. Dishonest state government officials misled the Oneidas and cheated them out of their property. First, officials would offer to rent Oneida land. Then, after the Oneidas had agreed, the officials would claim that they had actually *bought* the land.

The Oneidas asked the federal government for help in recovering their stolen land. But their requests were ignored. Gradually, the Oneidas were forced out of their homeland. Many resettled in Wisconsin and Canada.

For centuries, the Oneida homeland had covered some six million acres. By the early 1900s, the Oneidas controlled only 32 acres of the land that had originally belonged to them.

Conclusion

For two centuries, the Oneidas' heroism was nearly forgotten. However, the Indian nation has recently received new recognition. Public gatherings at Revolutionary War battlefields have celebrated the Oneidas' important role.

The Oneidas stepped forward at a critical moment in American history. Their courage helped the United States win its independence. Long ago, America's leaders promised, "While the sun and moon continue to give light to the world, we shall love and respect you." Today, that friendship is finally being honored again.

Returning Home

Today, some Oneidas are returning home. Leaders of the Indian nation have bought several thousand acres that were once Oneida homeland in New York State. There, they have built housing, a health clinic, and a thriving cultural center.

Responding

Sequence of Events By the
early 1900s, the Oneidas had lost almost all of their
land. What sequence of events led to the loss of
their land? Copy and complete the chart below.

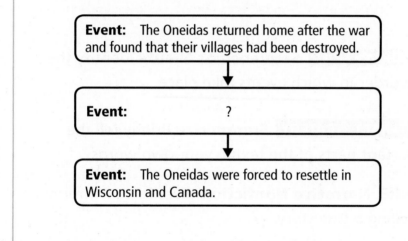

Event: The Oneidas returned home after the war
and found that their villages had been destroyed.

Event: ?

Event: The Oneidas were forced to resettle in
Wisconsin and Canada.

Write About It

Text to World The People of the Long House held
discussions to settle their internal disagreements.
Think of rules you know for settling disagreements.
Write a paragraph explaining those rules.

apprentice	dexterity
aspects	influential
authorities	persuade
bondage	provisions
contributions	tentative

✓ **TARGET SKILL** **Sequence of Events** Identify the time order in which events take place.

✓ **TARGET STRATEGY** **Summarize** Briefly tell the important parts of the text in your own words.

GENRE **Narrative Nonfiction** gives factual information by telling a true story.